Making a Bug Habitat

by Natalie Lunis

Table of Contents

What Can You Learn by Watching Bugs?. 2

How Do You Make a Bug Habitat?. 8

What Can You Learn by Watching Bugs?

Bugs live in many places.
You can learn a lot by watching them.

There are many different kinds of bugs.
Some are small. Some are big.

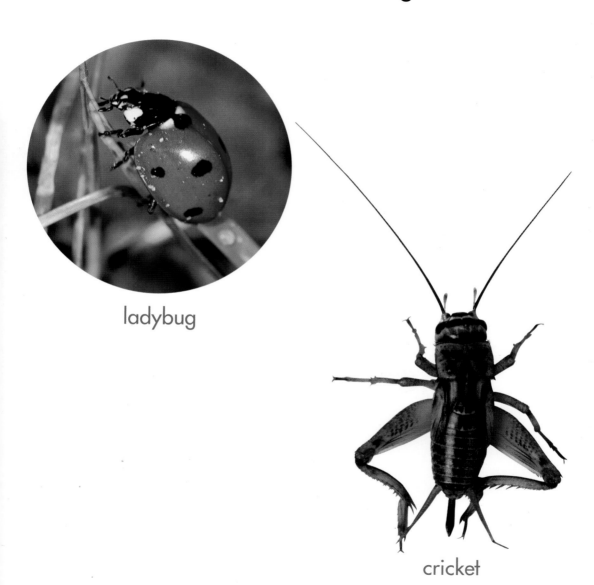

ladybug

cricket

Some bugs are easy to see.
Other bugs are hard to see.

butterfly

katydid

Some bugs fly. Other bugs do not.

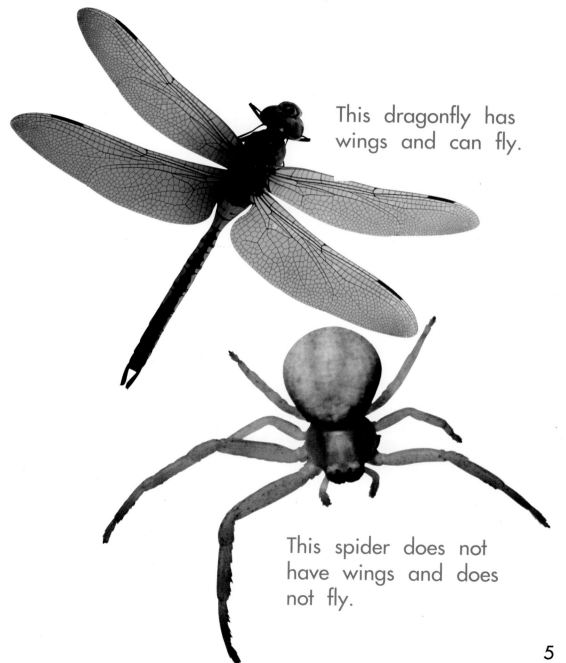

This dragonfly has wings and can fly.

This spider does not have wings and does not fly.

Some bugs feed on flowers.
Other bugs eat leaves or grass.
Some bugs eat other bugs.

Honeybees collect and eat pollen from flowers.
Ladybugs eat tiny insects that live on plants.
Caterpillars eat leaves.

A habitat is the place where an animal lives. You can find a bug and make a habitat for it. You can watch the bug up close in the habitat you make.

grasshopper

How Do You Make a Bug Habitat?

Here are the things you will need:

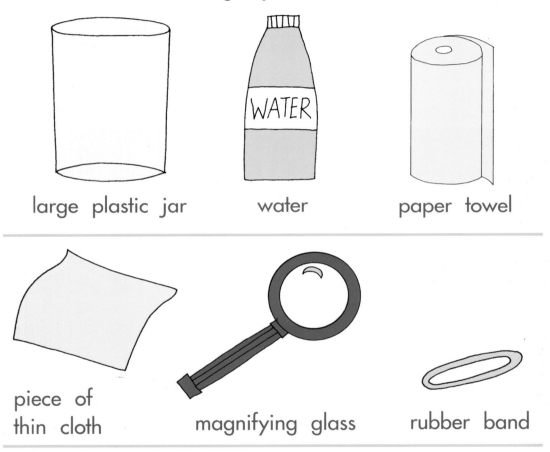

large plastic jar   water   paper towel

piece of
thin cloth   magnifying glass   rubber band

You will also need a pencil and paper.
You can use them to draw and write about
what you see.

Step 1 Go outside and look for a bug for your habitat. You might look in a garden, on a lawn, or under a rock.

Step 2 Make sure that the bug is safe to touch. Here are some bugs that are safe to touch.

beetle

praying mantis

Here are some bugs that are not safe to touch. These bugs can bite or sting.

bumblebee

fly

If you are not sure if a bug bites or stings, do not touch it.

Step 3 Once you have found a bug for your habitat, watch it for a while.

Try to answer these questions:
- What kind of place does the bug like?
- How wet or dry is the place?
- What kinds of leaves, sticks, or soil are around?

Step 4 Make a home for your bug. Get some leaves, sticks, or soil from the place it likes. Put these in the jar.

Step 5 Wet a small sheet of paper towel and put it in the jar, too.

WATER

Step 6 Put your bug in the jar.

Step 7 Use the cloth and the rubber band to cover the jar.

Step 8 Use the magnifying glass to take a close look at your bug. What do you see that you could not see before?

Step 9 Watch your bug to see how it acts.

Try to answer these questions:
- How does the bug move?
- Does it eat anything that you put in the habitat?
- Does it drink water from the paper towel?

Step 10 Take your bug back to the place where you found it. Let it go. Now it can live in its real habitat again.

Write down what you learned about your bug.